OASIS OF POERTY

IN A WORLD FULL OF MIRAGES

SUSANNA CELSIA

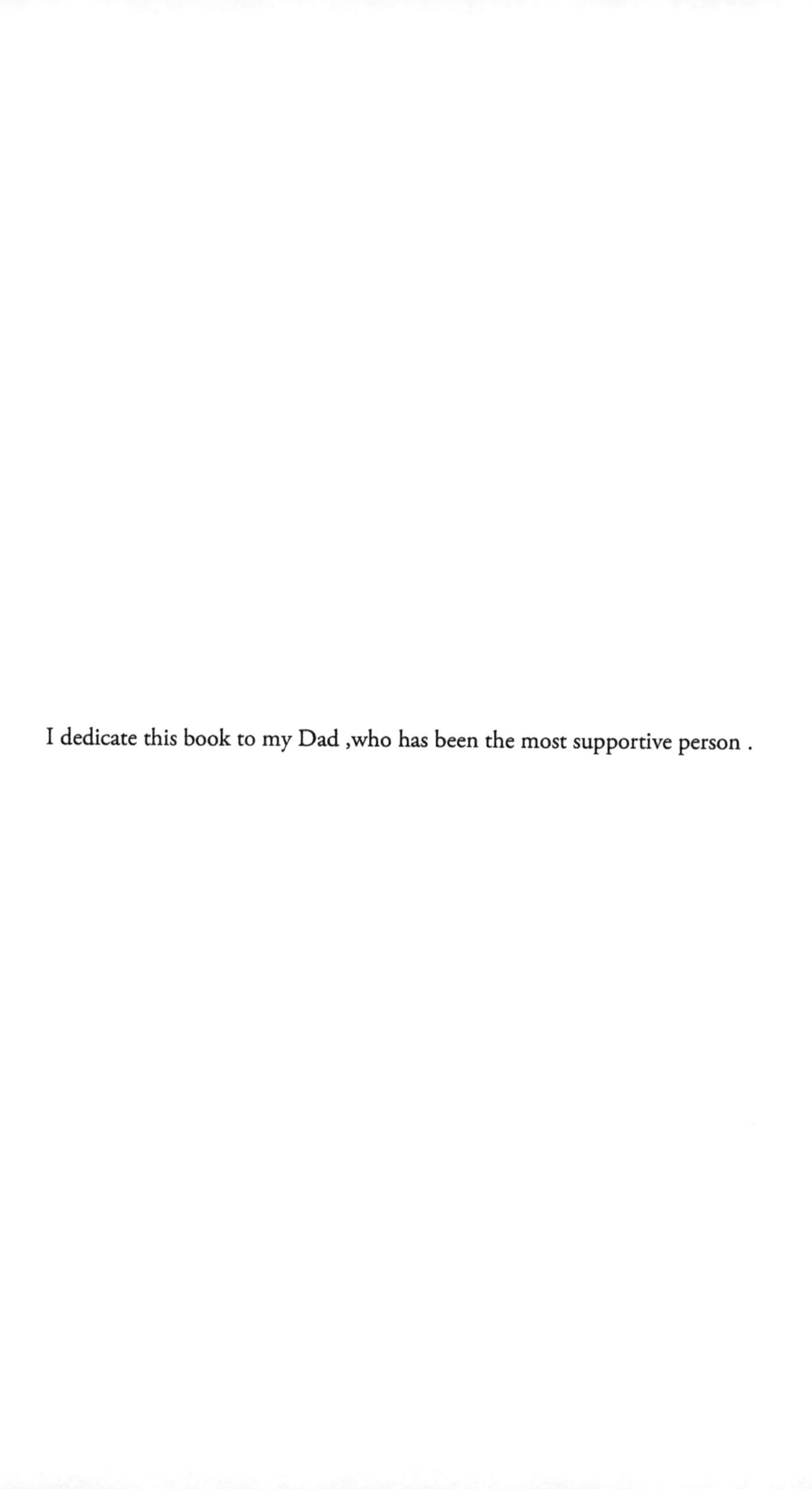

I dedicate this book to my Dad ,who has been the most supportive person .

Contents

Contents

1. RONITA (Caged bird melodies)

The caged bird melodies…
These strong bars all around me, I try to free myself day and night.
In my every attempt my beautiful feathers just fly away .
Those beautiful feathers in golden and red ,better than the fabrics of the merchants of Arabia.
The color of my wings, so rich and unfading. Better than the Chief's camel's cloack.
As every asset of golden and red fall of me....My heart aches With my heart, my arms ache as I hold these strong iron bars.
I pull and push and try so hard, just to grow weaker and weary.
I turn in circles, in this bronze plated iron cage.
Oh !the slaves of the King and maidens of the Queen,
Can you stop by?! and hear the melodies of the caged bird.
Shes on the branch ,singing a different song "Ronita ronita" I sit here holding these bars, my eyes weary and I'm so weak,but can pick up the note …
The sad notes of the songs of the lonley bird She sings, she hops its "ronita ronita" Touch my heart feel the beat. Feel my weary soul.
Wish I could sing"ronita ronita" I could lose anything!!
But my hope I would never lose!!
that some day I would be free, and will join her and sing"ronita ronita"
I can see the sunlight again and not just the reflection of the queens mirrored dress.

And will happily hop around saying "ronita ronita" Dont loose hope
no matter what you loose.
We parrots aren't meant to say what you want us to say!!
But fly high saying "ronita ronita"

2. FACT VS TRUTH

The fact is that, I'm on the hill of difficulty .
I'm falling ,holding on to the rugged rock.
Mud all over me ! these hard rocks have torn my flesh .
With bleeding wounds and torn clothes and rough hands I hold on o the rock.
The fact is that ,I'm in pain.
The fact is that, I'm struggling to climb up the hill .
The fact is that I'm all wounded and low, but the truth is that, I'm in progress , a happy pilgrim , the truth is that, I'm more than a conqueror
The fact is that, I'm all alone , fighting the toughest battles all alone .
The fact is that ,I'm a wounded soldier fighting for life .
The fact is that, I'm discouraged , broken and bruised but the truth is that ,.
I'm a solider I wear an armor and I'm in progress.
More than a conqueror, moving forward.
The truth is I'm in progress, a happy pilgrim.
I'm victorious, moving closer to the celestial city.
The fact is that ,I'm in a dark valley ,
the valley of shadow of death.
The fact is that, I hear scary sounds and whispers of discouragement .
The fact is that, I see nothing but darkness everywhere.
But the truth is that I'm moving forward.
I'm in progress, a happy pilgrim, moving forward and closer to the celestial city .

Facts remain facts, but the Truth is all that matters

3. WARRIOR

Shes a woman
,but a warrior.
Battles do not terrify her, she is trained for battle.
She fights every battle, that comes by her way.
she faces the enemy head on, doesn't turn back.
Her teeth thresh mountains, crushes and brings them to nothing.
She ties her hair, wears her armour, fixes her eyes, looks at the battlefield, Plans for war.
Her feet so strong.
Her face so bold.
She runs with all her might.
Faces her enemy, Threshes him Crushes him And brings him to nothing.
Her wounds open, Her arms bleeding
She wipes of her blood like it was sweat,
and continues to fight Battle after battle she faces,
but that only makes her stronger and her trains her arms more.
Can you hear the war cry ???
She is not just a woman ,but a warrior Can you hear the sound of victory???
She has won the battle!!
She doesn't give up. She is never afraid!
The mighty warrior is her king,
Who can stand against her ??

Chapter4

Shes on the floor,
laying with her face to the ground.
Drenching the royal carpet ,with tears.
She is in sack clothes.
Her crown fallen to a corner, The royal pillow ,of her crown empty.
Her maids don't speak a word, ready to help her in every way .
Just waiting for her command , but she won't move.
Her royal bed all set and ready, ornamented with purple and stones.
But she wont leave the ground.
Her throne waiting to be enthroned.
Her ministers sad and cold. waiting for the crown to rule again.
Waiting for her stern and sweet face, with royalty and power.
She rules with her royal scepter .
That one day , did the Queen forget that she was a"" Queen".
Did she forget the promises and power she was given, when she took her scepter for the very first time .
She ran ….threw her purple and fur .
Broke down in to tears and never built up again .
Her kingdom breaking down , the walls crumbling down , enemies rejoicing around
. No one to built it up , Her people fighting, killing and rioting.
The woman and children hungry and crying, Longing and wailing saying "Queen come back !!!
Crying and fighting and hitting the palace doors, "We need our Queen back" Darling , won't you get up? And take up your place .

Wipe up your tears ,you have a kingdom to care Dry up your tears ,nothing has really changed .
Your kingdom is waiting for you to be enthroned.
You are Queen with a kingdom to rule , have a province to care , with woman and children and loyal people to care .
Fix yr crown.
Take your sceptre.
Take your place.
Take heart.
Nothing ever changed,
Never forget your position and potential and authority.
you are born to rule ,young Queen .
She gets up , her maids hold her arms.
Takes her royal mirror studded with pearls.
She looks into her eyes and says … "you were born to rule ,no heartbreak can take away your place and who you are" .
She walks down, Gathering all her courage she looks at her kingdom… "you will be rebuilt" she whispers . She takes her sceptre and takes back her place .
Her eyes say" no heartbreak can change the authority and royalty I posses ".

Chapter5

Dreams are tangible at the right time in the right place.
It could be at that moment of devastation in the deepest waters,
fighting the currents and pushing through the depth to touch that beautiful pearl
It could be at the coldest nights .
When you battled every height and your burden wasn't light.
When your numb heart , starts feeling …. That beautiful moment,
its magical when numbness slowly heals ,
as your cheek gets numb when the cold wind strikes.
On the steepest mountains .
It could be after that freezing night ,
you dont want to remember but can never forget ,
that freezing lake when you tried to swim,
and your arms were weak and you couldn't swim ,
you held on to that piece of wood it felt like it was holy grail ,
that night so hard .
your thoughts din't really matter.
Rescuers is all you wanted
but you had to fight it on your own .
The moonlight din't really matter … although it did matter on that happy night when,
you walked across this beautiful bridge looked at the shimmering moon ,
could feel the ray of hope as two lights from the inside and out collide .

Now it's not the same it's the toughest of days .
But the morning did break through !
you saw the sun rising.
Your heart is pounding
, you felt strong arms holding your weak hands and pulling you out .
That moment when you know your alive.
Your feet touches the land ,
you feel the sunlight on your skin ....
and your heart tells "you are ok !" And your mind ,still doesn't know
if your dreaming
It could be like touching an oasis , and you still feels it's a mirage.
You can't believe that it's not a mirage .
The nights for the guards at the big bronze doors ,
when every second feels like an hour , every hour feels like a day
Alertness with shrewdness should he have ,
weary and tierdness hits him like a wave .
No matter how long it takes ,
dawn is not afar, so is your dream season

Chapter6

The Story of Invention Why does the sun rise,
what makes the fields bloom.
The sea roars with its might ,
does the moon govern you I wonder
,do you try to reach the moon rising up so high when it's not to be seen.
Rivers I see.
Why dont the clouds disappear I wonder .
Is it nature's Laws
.The unending quest!Aristotle wondered. Athens reasoned.
Am I standing on flat ground questioned Magellan
The vast space around me ,
how vast,how much,how far.
Is it nature's Laws ?The Unending Quest!
The quest maybe unending,but the discoveries are true about
The laws of nature that's ruling over you .
How small ,smaller,minute and nano can particles be.
Is there a world my eyes can't see .
Are there sounds around me that my ears can't hear,
the ultrasounds indeed.
Staring at the sea looking at waves rise as the breeze hits my face .
I say a word can it cross the seas and reach the other corner ,thought great minds.
Is it natures laws .
The unending quest! How could everything sustain.

How do living creatures move.
What could this invincible,incredible thing be Can we obtain this Holy Grail.
Is it the Laws of energy .
Never ending Quest.
How could I think of all this. How could I discover and invent,what could this invincible thing be. Can I make an artificial me,can I rule over the rules. Can I make my own Laws . Can I end the Quest ,Artificial Intelligenlce indeed.

7. HAVE EVERYTHING BUT NOTHING

Little miss tiny ,
grew up to shiny .
She went for a walk, and found a shop out of stock!
She asked him for a lolly,
and he answered sorry.
This is a market ! But has nothing but empty pocket
Oh! She marvelled Until she was startled,
by the miss world, whose outfits stole the girl.
But whose charm, disturbed the calm.
As she shone with black,
With yellow spots around her neck ,
Well,she resembled a crow !
What a splendid gown ,
on a skinny little brown, ugly witch!
Hear the trumpets pitch , Oh! It's a bassoon .
Here come the maids, On the red carpet.
All the crowd in the market ,
follow the kinsmen .
Where is the bride? She wondered then
I walked through ,gold plated gates,
I wondered if it was a bait ? I was astonished by the crockery ,
Well, now mine seemed like a house of mockery .
I went through the delicate screens,
As I entered the room that made me scream.

Alas! What is my eyes seeing ,
A woman screaming ,
with pain and mourning "Oh! Why is it morning !!"
I went beside her with fear And questioned with shiver ,
Are you alright ??
She repliedWell ,
what happened ?
It all started,
when I was adolescent, I was wonderful as incent .
Until the day I became jealous ,
I started working zealous .
To build a huge palace ,
where I would be the princess.
Wealth I gained, health I lost .
I was not content with God's gift ,
but longed for my wishlist .
And hence spoilt my health ,
that God gifted me as wealth.
The bible says your body is the temple of God,
but I turned into a temple of demons by my odd, lustful implementations,
I though life has no limitations
. But alas !Im like a shop without goods,
An ugly witch who reads the moons, with a pretty gown
oh! I am sinking down Little miss thinks "How can one have everything but nothing

8. Mr.Pete

Mr .Pete swept and swept until he sat and wept .
As the sun rises ,
The city has broomstick crises.
But Mr.Pete swept and swept , until he sat and wept .
Why did he weep ? did any crazy creature creep ??
well it was the citizens of Verona that caused him a trauma .
Clean and tidy was Verona's maze,
that Mr.Pete would sit and gaze.
The next instant the maze Triggered Mr.Pete to craze ,
It was littered and cluttered all over As the citizens of Verona went over.
Mr Pete swept and swept until he sat and wept .
Mr.Pete jumped with joy as everything was tidy,
But in the wink of the eye ,wrappers filled the city .
The candy man just passed And the tidy night dint last .
Mr.Pete swept and swept until he sat and wept .
He always sowed with tears
he never reaped a pear .
although he was a spark, he could never ignite a bark
well , would he ignite a forest? but he was literally modest
Mr. Pete swept and swept until he sat and wept

9. BE WHAT YOU OUGHT TO BE

A drop of poison, can change ones feast, into ones last fleet.
A pinch of yeast can change the dough which is least, into plenty that satisfies.
A tiny lens magnifies. a tiny little light, makes darkness run with fright.
Oh!! Is Rambo in life today, that's what you ought to be someday.
Maybe single in count, but one man army on mount.
What if the sun doesn't shine?? saying the surrounding is like brine!
Each one has a duty to perform.
Despite their unique form.
What if the dead don't decompose ?
What would the earth compose? Every creature is shouldered by a load of cares.
Well,we are often filled with nightmares Despite the scary scenes We got to work for our means.
Live what you preach , so that you may reach. Be a wordless book.
But touch every corner and nook. Be selfless, to lose less.
Be humble So that you don't stumble.

10. CLICHÉ

She walks down the stairs, she takes a turn, everyone takes a turn,
and say " oh my , hold me ! my head is taking a turn".
He drops the books from his hands down, and is speechless, as his
heart beat says. "can anything in this universe define beauty better
than you “.
She flaunts her hair that’s brownish red
.It smells like the meadows of the spring.. her clothes fitting her
perfectly ,
all the girls turn away with jealousy and whisper how could she?...
what does she eat?... .how could she work out?....
She gives a look with long eyelashes and attractive eyes .
Green as an apple from my grandpa’s orchard are her eyes
. Her skin shines , as the light from the window falls on her even skin
!!
How beautiful!!but how is it possible?!
whereas I have a patched mat say the girls.
The Jean’s so skinny , how do her legs fit inside of those...shes
beautiful!! Says the world .
As she walks down the stairs with her high heels with the sound they
make . Its 10 PM she opens her apartment door ,
runs to her bed takes of those painful things off her legs groans with
pain .
She takes her lenses off and looks into her black pupils as she leans
across the dressing table ,
takes off her makeup as her body demands for sleep ,

as she wipes of every layer her epidermis says wow we can finally breath !!!
As she takes of those eyelashes she says "at the end of the day your not mine".
She changes to her t-shirt and groans with pain, as her organs say finally say we have space!!!
We ain't crushed any more !!
Her nerves say ,those strong denim arms have finally left!!
When they celebrate they also cry as their enemy would be back again !!
And they hear the terrifying news that their enemies are prone to invade and stay here forever ..
Wrinkles is kocking the door as all her relatives are there concealer is her sister and foundation her aunt
A lot of powerful kingdoms are planning to invade Ms beautiful as she has given shelter to a lot of foreign spies .If beautiful is this.. from where have we learnt it ??!!
Is it a cliche indeed?
Beautiful is she who maintains the beauty she was born with .
Strengthens her kingdom fights against the spies and invaders .
We cant let this be a cliche anymore

Printed by Libri Plureos GmbH in Hamburg, Germany